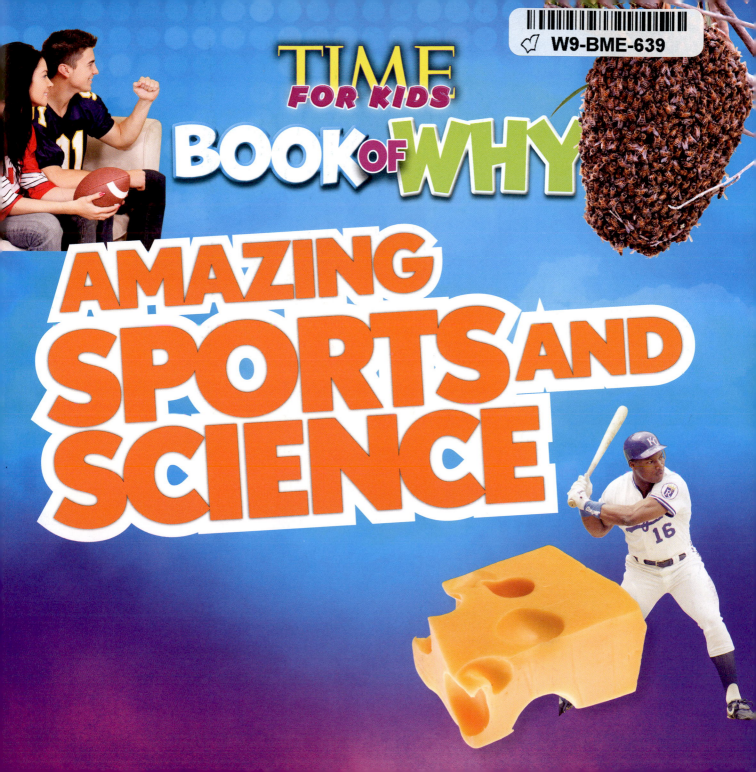

TIME FOR KIDS
BOOK OF WHY

AMAZING SPORTS AND SCIENCE

TIME FOR KIDS

Managing Editor: Nellie Gonzalez Cutler
Editor: Brenda Iasevoli
Creative Director: Jennifer Kraemer-Smith

Time Home Entertainment

Publisher: Jim Childs
Vice President, Brand &
Digital Strategy: Steven Sandonato
Executive Director, Marketing Services: Carol Pittard
Executive Director, Retail & Special Sales: Tom Mifsud
Executive Publishing Director: Joy Bomba
Director, Bookazine Development
& Marketing: Laura Adam
Vice President, Finance Director: Vandana Patel
Publishing Director: Megan Pearlman
Assistant General Counsel: Simone Procas
Assistant Director, Special Sales: Ilene Schreider
Brand Manager: Jonathan White
Associate Prepress Manager: Alex Voznesenskiy
Associate Production Manager: Kimberly Marshall
Associate Project Manager: Stephanie Braga

Editorial Director: Stephen Koepp
Senior Editor: Roe D'Angelo
Copy Chief: Rina Bander
Design Manager: Anne-Michelle Gallero
Editorial Operations: Gina Scauzillo

Special thanks: Katherine Barnet, Brad Beatson, Jeremy Biloon, Susan Chodakiewicz, Rose Cirrincione, Assu Etsubneh, Mariana Evans, Christine Font, Susan Hettleman, Hillary Hirsch, David Kahn, Amy Mangus, Nina Mistry, Dave Rozzelle, Ricardo Santiago, Adriana Tierno

Copyright © 2010 Time for Kids Big Book of WHY
Copyright © 2014 Time Home Entertainment Inc.
All TIME FOR KIDS material © 2014 by Time Inc.
TIME FOR KIDS and the red border design are registered trademarks of Time Inc.

Contents of this book previously appeared in Time For Kids Big Book of WHY.

For information on TIME FOR KIDS magazine for the classroom or home, go to TIMEFORKIDS.COM or call 1-800-777-8600.
For subscriptions to SI KIDS, go to SIKIDS.COM or call 1-800-889-6007.

Published by TIME FOR KIDS Books,
An imprint of Time Home Entertainment Inc.
135 West 50th Street
New York, NY 10020

ISBN 10: 1-60320-986-7
ISBN 13: 978-1-60320-986-1

TIME FOR KIDS is a trademark of Time Inc.

We welcome your comments and suggestions about TIME FOR KIDS Books. Please write to us at:
TIME FOR KIDS Books, Attention: Book Editors, P.O. Box 11016, Des Moines, IA 50336-1016
If you would like to order any of our hardcover Collector's Edition books, please call us at1-800-327-6388 (Monday through Friday, 7 a.m. to 8 p.m., or Saturday, 7 a.m. to 6 p.m., Central Time).

1 QGT 14

Picture credits

t = top, b = bottom, c = center,
r = right, l = left

Front and Back cover:
Baseball with Red Stitching: 104661557, thinkstock.com
Chemistry Vials: McCarony, shutterstock.com
Molecule: Natykach Natalila, shutterstock.com
Football PLayer: RTimages, shutterstock.com
Soccer Player: 121034522, thinkstock.com
Basketball: Neyro, shutterstock.com
Hot Peppers: Maks Narodenko, shutterstock.com
Race Horses: Mikhail Pogosov, shutterstock.com
Racehorse: Margo Harrison, shutterstock.com

Contents Page:
Ooyoo/Istockphoto, Lick Observatory/NASA, Gene Chutka/Istockphoto, Digitalsport/Shutterstock Photoagency

Inside:
AFP: 6t.

AP Photo: Gene J. Puskar: 7t, 34t, David Duprey: 8l, 10br, Harry Harris: 14b, 20tl, Kathy Willens: 20b, 21b, Kathy Willens: 25r.

Bigstock: Warren Rosenberg: 34b.

Corbis: Gideon Mendel/In Pictures: 31.

Dreamstime: Alexandre Fagundes De Fagundes: 4b, Mashe: 6b, Tomislav Birtic: 13l, Rob Corbett: 14t, Amy Myers: 15b, Yuri Arcurs: 30t, Ovidiu Iordache: 41b.

Fotolia: Melany Dieterle: 30b.

Getty Images: Shaun Botterill/Getty Images Sport: 5l, Clive Mason: 11b, Gene Lower/Getty Images Sport: 13r, Chris McGrath/Getty Images Sport: 17b, Ron Vesely: 20tr, Focus on Sport: 21t, Pictorial Parade/Archive Photos: 23tr, Racing One/ISC Archives: 26, Focus on Sport: 27l, Ragnar Schmuck: 42t.

Rex Features: Everett Collection: 12b, Canadian Press: 25l, Giuliano Bevilacqua: 27r.

IOC: 5r.

Istockphoto: Ooyoo: 29t, urafoc: 33b, Brett Lamb Graphics: 35, Kieran Mithani: 42b, Gene Chutka: 44, 45.

Library of Congress Prints and Photographs Division, Washington, D.C.: 12t.

NASA: Lick Observatory: 40t, 40b.

Photolibrary: Mike Kemp: 8r, The Print Collector: 17t.

Reuters: Tim Shaffer: 7l, Todd Korol: 18, Darren Staples: 28b.

Shutterstock: Eugene Buchko: 4t, 48, Doug James: 9, Digitalsport Photoagency: 10t, Doug James: 10bl, Ilja Masik: 11t, Pavel Ignatov: 15t, Marty Ellis: 16, Pinkcandy: 19, Brandon Parry: 22t, Rui Alexandre Araujo: 22b, Herbert Kratky: 23l, Michael Pettigrew: 23cr, Jacqueline Abromeit: 24l, Cynoclub: 24r, Svand: 28t, Kellie L. Folkerts: 29b, Steve Cukrov: 32t, 47, Nataliya Peregudova: 32b, Jan Van Der Hoeven: 33t, Valentyn Volkov: 36t, Gelpi: 36b, Tischenko Irina: 37l, Vibrant Image Studio: 37r, Adventure Stock: 38t, Brykaylo Yuriy: 38b, Kitch Bain: 39t, Frontpage: 39b, Iphotos: 41t, Dmitriy Shironosov: 43t, Goodluz: 43b

Q2AMedia Art Bank: 18, 31

CONTENTS & QUESTIONS

Here's a look at some of the questions inside.

Why are baseball fields different sizes?

Not all baseball fields are the same size. While the rules of Major League Baseball spell out the exact size of the infield, the outfield is a different story. Each ballpark has different dimensions. According to the rules, the distance from home plate to the nearest fence in fair territory must be 250 feet (76.2 m) or more. Some teams use their field's measurements to their advantage. The Yankees often put strong left-handed hitters in the lineup to hit more home runs over Yankee Stadium's short right-field fence. The Red Sox fill their lineup with right-handed hitters to clear the close-by left-field fence at Fenway Park.

WHY WERE FOOTBALL FIELDS' SIZE CHANGED FROM 110 YARDS TO 100 YARDS?

Only infields in baseball parks have the same dimensions.

The dimensions of American football fields are the same: 100 yards (91.44 m) from one goal line to the other. American football fields used to be 110 yards (100.58 m) long. The size of the field gradually changed over the years because some of the rules changed.

WHY WAS THE ZAMBONI MACHINE INVENTED?

In the early 1940s, Frank Zamboni had a cool idea for ice skating rinks. He wanted to make a machine that made ice smooth in minutes. Skaters' blades made grooves and bumps in the ice on rinks. Workers had to shovel away ice shavings and spray water, which froze and filled the grooves, making the ice smooth. This took more than an hour. Frank Zamboni's machine did the job faster. Today, the Zamboni is used at most ice rinks.

Who was the **first woman** on a **Wheaties Box** ?

The makers of Wheaties like to say their cereal is the "Breakfast of Champions." But for many years, all the champions that appeared on Wheaties boxes were men. That all changed in 1935, when Olympic track and field star Babe Didrikson became the first woman to appear on the a Wheaties box. At the time, the athletes—male or female— appeared only on the side of the box, not the cover. In 1984, Olympic gymnast Mary Lou Retton became the first woman to appear on the cover of the box.

Charlotte Cooper won a gold medal in tennis at the 1900 Olympic Games.

Tara Lipinski is the youngest woman to win an Olympic gold medal in figure skating.

WHEN DID WOMEN START COMPETING IN THE OLYMPICS?

Women began taking part in the Olympic Games for the first time in 1900. The Games were held in Paris, France. There were 22 women who participated that year. A Mrs. Brohy and a Miss Ohnier of France were the first to compete. They played croquet.

WHO WERE THE YOUNGEST WOMEN TO WIN OLYMPIC GOLD MEDALS?

At 13 years of age, Kim Yun-Mi of South Korea became the youngest Olympic gold-medal winner of all time. Kim was a member of the South Korean short-track speed skating relay team. That team won the women's 3,000-meter relay at the 1994 Winter Games. The youngest female to win an individual gold medal in the Winter Olympics is Tara Lipinski of the U.S. She won the gold in figure skating at the age of 15 in 1998.

Curling is like shuffleboard on ice.

What is the sport of curling?

Curling is one of the most popular sports in the world. It is similar to shuffleboard, except that curling is played on ice. Players slide a 42-pound (19 kg) stone disc toward a painted target on the ice to knock the opponent's stone out of the target area. Curling gets its name from the way the rock slides in a curl down the ice.

Why is fishing called angling?

When people go fishing, they use hooks. Hooks are known as angles because of their curved shapes. If you use a hook rather than a net to fish, you're an angler.

If you fish with a pole, you're an angler!

Why is a basketball **hoop 10 feet off the ground?**

Ten feet (3.05 m) is how high James Naismith put the hoops when he invented basketball. Naismith created the sport in 1891 by attaching peach baskets to two handrails in the spectators' gallery at the local YMCA in Springfield, Massachusetts. Each basket was 10 feet off the ground. The sport has kept the same basket height ever since.

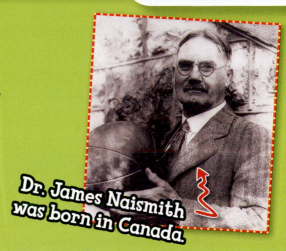

Dr. James Naismith was born in Canada.

WHY DO SOME PEOPLE CALL BASKETBALL PLAYERS "CAGERS"?

In the early days of the sport, the first team to put a hand on a ball that flew into the stands was given possession of the ball. When the ball went off the court, the players rushed for it, and fans often got hurt. To keep the ball in play at all times and to stop the accidents, someone decided to put a cage around the court. That's why basketball players are known as "cagers." The cages were removed in the 1920s, when the out-of-bounds rule was changed. The new rule: when the ball goes out of bounds, play stops and the team that didn't touch the ball last is given possession.

Jump shots are the most important shots in basketball.

HOW DID THE JUMP SHOT BECOME SO POPULAR IN BASKETBALL?

Before there was a jump shot, the set shot ruled. Players planted their feet on the court and shot the ball with one or both hands. Some players wanted to find a better way to score. As the game changed, players eventually developed the jump shot. In a jump shot, a player jumps in the air to make it more difficult for a defender on the other team to block the shot. The best jump shooters do not jump very high, however. It's more important to shoot quickly, when the defender does not expect the player with the ball to shoot.

7

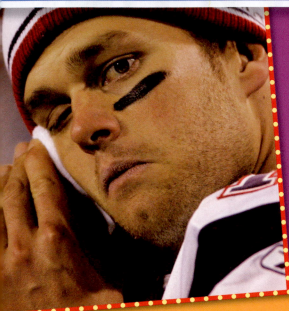

Why do football players put **black grease under their eyes?**

Football players put black grease under their eyes to make it easier to see the ball. The black grease is made mostly of wax and cuts down the sun's glare. Players began wearing the grease in the 1940s. They burned the end of a cork, let it cool, and used it to color their cheek bones black. Today, some players wear anti-glare stickers under their eyes.

WHY DO SOME FOOTBALL PLAYERS TAPE THEIR FINGERS?

College and pro football players often tape their fingers, believing the tape will make their grips stronger. However, a scientific study found that there was no difference in the grip strength of players whose fingers were taped and players whose fingers were not taped.

Why do football coaches wear headsets?

Football coaches wear headsets so they can talk to their assistant coaches who are sitting high above the field. Those coaches have a bird's-eye view of the game. They can see where mistakes are being made and can also tell which plays might work best. The coaches in the stands pass information to the coach on the field, who then passes it on to the team's quarterback or defense.

Why do race cars run on bald tires?

Tire treads—the pattern of deep grooves on the tires—make a car slower because of increased **friction** between the tire and the road. That's why race car tires are bald. In NASCAR races, smooth car tires allow for more speed. They have to be changed four to five times during a race.

WHAT PART DOES AERODYNAMICS PLAY IN RACE CAR DRIVING?

You can't talk about car racing without talking about **aerodynamics**, the study of how air flows over a surface. There are two major forces created by a car's movement. The first is drag. Drag is the resistance a car has when passing through air at high speeds. Drag takes away some of the car's power and speed. The second major force is called downforce. Downforce is air pressure pushing directly down on a car. Downforce helps the car grip the road.

WHY DO RACE CAR DRIVERS TAILGATE?

Race car drivers have perfected a racing technique called drafting. This is the aerodynamic effect that allows a tailgating car to move faster than the car in front. How does that happen? The lead car whizzes down the track, pushing the air in front out of the way. That opens a gap of air between the lead car and the second car. As the second car drives into the gap, not much air resistance pushes on its front end. So, the second car can move faster and save fuel.

Drafting allows race cars to go faster.

Why do some **race cars** have "wings"?

In car racing, the faster a car travels the greater its lift, or tendency to rise. When lift becomes too great, it causes the car to lose its grip on the road, making it hard to control. Race cars have wing-shaped parts called spoilers to fight off this lift. The spoilers create a downward force, which helps keep the car on the road.

spoiler

WHAT MAKES NASCAR CARS BETTER THAN THE "OLD" STOCK CARS?

Long ago, NASCAR drivers would "soup up" street cars and race them on a track. Today, NASCAR autos are wonders of science. Millions of dollars go into planning and designing them. Experts use computers to create the fastest NASCAR auto shapes and engines for the track.

WHY DO RACE CARS HAVE ROLL CAGES?

Race car drivers sit in metal roll cages made to protect them from crashes and rollovers. There are many different roll cage designs.

Old-time stock cars were not as fast as today's models.

HOW CAN SNOWBOARDERS DO SO MANY FANCY TRICKS?

Snowboarders can do many tricks because of friction. They shift, or move, their weight to have less contact with the snow on one side of the board, and to have more contact with the snow on the other side of the board. They also slide down the snow so fast that it gives them the power to jump and twist in the air.

Science plays an important role in snowboarding.

Why do skiers wax their skis?

Wax on the bottom of a snow ski or snowboard allows it to slide down the slope with as little **friction** as possible. This means a skier can travel faster.

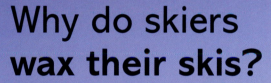

Why do bobsledders push their sleds?

The faster a bobsled team pushes its bobsled at the start of their run, the more momentum the sled has. Momentum reduces the impact of air and friction on the moving sled, so it will go faster. Saving even one-tenth of a second during the start of a race can save one-third of a second on the entire bobsled run—the difference between winning and losing.

Did Abner Doubleday invent baseball?

People have been arguing for years about the origins of baseball. According to legend, Abner Doubleday invented the game in Cooperstown, New York, in 1839. Doubleday, however, never claimed he invented the game. A special panel in 1908, made up of baseball officials, gave Doubleday credit. If Doubleday didn't invent baseball, then who did? It's really anyone's guess.

Did Abner Doubleday invent baseball?

WHY DID THE BROOKLYN DODGERS HIRE JACKIE ROBINSON?

In 1947, when Branch Rickey, an executive with the Brooklyn Dodgers, hired Jackie Robinson, baseball's color line was broken. When Rickey became the Dodgers' general manager in 1942, he quietly began plans to bring black players to the team. Rickey picked Robinson because he was a good player, and he knew Robinson would be strong enough to handle the pressure of being the first African American in the big leagues.

WHY DID IT TAKE SO LONG FOR AFRICAN AMERICANS TO PLAY MAJOR LEAGUE BASEBALL?

African Americans couldn't play in the major leagues due to discrimination and racism. Many owners and players didn't believe blacks should play on white teams. Owners also thought whites wouldn't come to watch blacks play. So, African Americans formed a league of their own—the Negro League. White owners of major league ball clubs then rented their stadiums to Negro League teams when the major league teams were on the road. If the teams were **integrated**, there would be no more Negro League—and then no one would rent the stadiums. This meant white owners would lose money.

When was the **first forward pass** thrown in football?

For years, rules kept players from passing the ball. When President Theodore Roosevelt met with college officials to make the game safer, they changed the rules to allow passing. In 1906, Bradbury Robinson, quarterback for Saint Louis University, tossed the football to teammate Jack Schneider. The defense was so surprised by the pass that Schneider just walked into the end zone to score. Soon, other teams began throwing forward passes.

How did the **Green Bay Packers** get their name?

The Green Bay Packers were first owned by a local meat-packing company called the Indian Packing Company. So, the team was named the Packers. The team was later owned by the Acme Packing Company. Although both companies went out of business, the name stayed.

WHY DO PLACEKICKERS SQUEEZE THE FOOTBALL?

Placekickers in football squeeze the football before they kick it to make it softer and rounder. They believe a new football does not travel as far as one that is softened up.

Where did the **World Series** get its name?

According to the *Baseball Almanac*, Major League Baseball had several championships during its early years. One, in 1884, was called the Championship of the United States. Newspapers named the winning team "world champions." The title stuck. In 1903, when Boston faced Pittsburgh in the championship series, people began calling it the World Series.

The New York Yankees show off the World Series trophy they won in 2009.

WHY IS BASEBALL'S NATIONAL LEAGUE CALLED THE SENIOR CIRCUIT?

There are two leagues in Major League Baseball—the National League and the American League. The National League was formed in 1876, and the American League began in 1901. Because the National League is older, people call it the Senior Circuit.

WHY DON'T AMERICAN LEAGUE PITCHERS BAT?

When Major League Baseball adopted Rule 6.10 in 1973, teams were allowed to designate, or choose, a player to bat in place of the pitcher (generally the weakest hitter on the team). That chosen player was known as the designated hitter, or DH for short. Today, the American League uses designated hitters, while the National League does not.

Ron Blomberg was baseball's first designated hitter.

Why does a curveball curve?

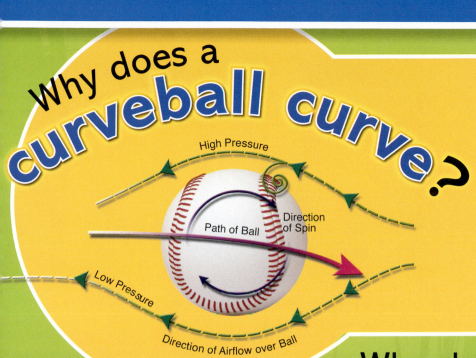

High Pressure

Path of Ball

Direction of Spin

Low Pressure

Direction of Airflow over Ball

A curveball moves to the right or left, and sometimes down. To throw a curve, a pitcher makes the ball spin sideways. As the spinning ball travels, low air pressure forms underneath it. The ball's stitching creates friction between the ball and the air. A high air pressure area forms on top of the ball, pushing the ball down to where the air pressure is the lowest. This imbalance causes the ball to curve toward one side.

WHY ARE ALUMINUM BATS MORE DANGEROUS THAN WOODEN BATS?

Many people say metal baseball bats are dangerous, especially for the pitcher on the opposing team. A ball flies off a metal bat faster than off a wooden bat. The faster the ball comes back to the pitcher, the less time the pitcher has to get out of the way, which can lead to injury.

Why do some youth baseball leagues use "soft" baseballs?

Many doctors advise young baseball players to use a soft type of baseball called a reduced injury factor (RIF) ball to protect their heads from serious injuries. The balls are the same size and weight as regular baseballs, but the inside of a RIF ball is made from a special foam. The foam can absorb more of an impact than a regular baseball if it should hit a player. This lessens the chances of getting hurt.

15

Why does a basketball bounce?

What happens when you try to dribble a basketball without any air in it? Nothing. Basketballs need pressurized air to bounce. Inside a basketball is a rubber pouch, or bladder. When that bladder is filled with air, it gives the ball a lot of **potential energy**. When the ball hits the ground, the air inside the ball compresses, or squeezes, as the skin of the ball flattens slightly at the bottom. Once the ball hits the floor and flattens, it bounces back. As the ball bounces, it returns to its original round shape.

Inflated basketballs have a lot of stored energy.

Why is a basketball orange?

Paul "Tony" Hinkle was a college basketball coach who invented the orange basketball. Until the late 1950s, basketballs were dark brown. Hinkle said fans and players had a hard time seeing the ball. He worked with the Spalding Company to come up with an orange-colored ball that was easier to see.

WHY DOES A BASKETBALL RIM HAVE A NET?

There are two reasons why basketball rims have nets. The first reason is that nets slow down balls that are going through baskets. Without a net, a ball would fly off in many directions. The second reason is that nets make it easier for players and fans to see if a shot goes through the basket.

Why were the first Olympics held?

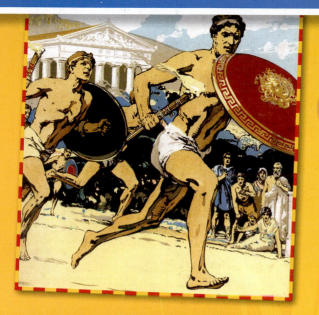

The first recorded Olympic Games were held in ancient Greece in 776 B.C., as a small festival to honor the god Zeus. The first Olympics had only a single event, a 210-yard (192 m) foot race called the *stadion*. The race took place in Olympia, in western Greece. The winner of that first race was a cook named Koroibos.

WHY DO OLYMPIC CHAMPIONS RECEIVE MEDALS?

The highest honor for any Olympic athlete is winning a gold medal. During the ancient Games, winners received olive wreaths to wear on their heads. The tradition of giving medals to the winners began at the Olympic Games in 1896. At that time, the winners who placed first did not get gold medals. Instead they received silver. Those who came in second took home a bronze medal, and third-place finishers received nothing.

WHY ARE THE OLYMPIC GAMES SOMETIMES CALLED AN OLYMPIAD?

An Olympiad was a four-year period that the ancient Greeks used to keep track of time. After the first Olympics were held, the Greeks held the Games every four years. That's why people refer to the Games as an Olympiad.

Olympic gold medals are mostly made of silver, with a bit of gold.

17

Why are there dimples on golf balls?

Golfers found out very early that scuffed-up golf balls fly farther than smooth balls. That's why there are between 300 and 500 dimples on a golf ball. Dimples give a golf ball lift—or height—by creating a layer of fast moving air on the top of the ball and a layer of slower moving air on the bottom of the ball.

Good golfers like Michelle Wie use the slice to their advantage.

CAN SOME GOLF BALLS FLY FARTHER THAN OTHER GOLF BALLS WHEN HIT THE SAME WAY?

How a golf ball is made impacts how far it will fly. One-piece balls are solid, with no layers. They are poorly made golf balls. A two-piece ball is tough and can also fly far. It has a solid core wrapped with a cover. Three-piece golf balls have rubber or liquid centers wrapped with elastic. Such balls create a large amount of spin, allowing a golfer to control the ball's flight when it is hit.

Two-piece ball

Three-piece ball

WHY DO GOLFERS "SLICE" THE BALL?

A slice is when the ball curves in the shape of a banana. Professional golfer Michelle Wie knows how to use the slice to get out of tough spots. She strikes the ball, causing it to spin sideways. Because Wie is right-handed, the ball starts heading left, and then swerves to the right. Wie and other golfers use the slice to hit around trees and ponds.

WHY DOES A SUPER BALL BOUNCE SO HIGH?

Super Balls are small, but they have a big bounce. That big bounce comes from compressing a hunk of synthetic, or human-made, rubber under a lot of pressure. Because the rubber is under so much pressure, it has a large amount of **potential energy**. That potential energy changes to kinetic energy when the ball bounces. As a result, a Super Ball bounces higher than an ordinary rubber ball.

Where did the **Hula-Hoop** idea come from?

Arthur "Spud" Melin and his friend, Richard Knerr, invented the Hula Hoop after they saw Australian children twirling wooden hoops around their waists. The pair gave their hip-swiveling plastic toy its famous name. The Hula-Hoop was a huge success for the toy company Wham-O. It sold 25 million hoops in the first four months of production in 1958.

What were the **first** Frisbees made of?

From 1871 until the 1950s, the Frisbie Baking Company of Bridgeport, Connecticut, sold pies to many New England colleges. Legend has it that a group of college students at Yale University in Connecticut took the empty tin pie plates—with the words "Frisbie's Pies" on them—and began tossing and catching them. In 1948, two men created a plastic version of a pie plate and called it a Pluto Platter. In 1957, Wham-O bought the rights to the Pluto Platter and soon changed the name to Frisbee in honor of the baking company that inspired the toy.

Which professional athletes have played more than two sports?

While many high school and college athletes have played more than one sport during the year, professional athletes usually play just one. There are exceptions, however. Bo Jackson was a running back for football's Los Angeles Raiders, and he also played baseball at different times for the Chicago White Sox, the California Angels, and the Kansas City Royals. Deion Sanders was another athlete who played pro football and baseball in the big leagues.

Bo Jackson played baseball and football.

In 2007, a Wagner T206 sold for $2.8 million.

WHICH ATHLETES HAVE PLAYED A PROFESSIONAL SPORT WITH ONE ARM?

The first one-armed pitcher to wear a baseball uniform was Pete Gray, who played for the St. Louis Browns. Gray's career was short-lived, however. When batting, he could not hit balls that curved because he had trouble stopping his swing with one arm. Jim Abbott, a stand-out pitcher, played with one arm for several teams, including the New York Yankees. Abbott was born without a right hand. After throwing the ball with his left hand, he quickly switched his glove—which was hanging on his right arm—to his left hand so he could catch the ball.

WHAT IS THE RAREST BASEBALL CARD?

A 1909 Honus Wagner T206 is the answer. Honus Wagner was a baseball player for the Pittsburgh Pirates. At that time, tobacco companies put baseball cards into their packages. Wagner didn't want his image used that way. When a tobacco company used his image without his permission, he stopped them from printing any more cards. Only a few had been made, making them very rare.

WHO WAS THE FIRST SUPER BOWL'S MOST VALUABLE PLAYER?

Green Bay Packer quarterback Bart Starr was named the Most Valuable Player of Super Bowl I when he led his team to victory over the Kansas City Chiefs. Starr completed 16 of 23 passes for 250 yards and three touchdowns.

When was the first Super Bowl held?

The Super Bowl began when the National Football League and American Football League got together to play a championship game. That was held on January 15, 1967, in Los Angeles, California. It was called the AFL-NFL Championship Game, later known as Super Bowl I. The Green Bay Packers beat the Kansas City Chiefs, 35-10.

Where did the Super Bowl get its name?

Lamar Hunt, the one-time owner of the Kansas City Chiefs, saw his daughter playing with a Super Ball. Suddenly, a light bulb went off in Hunt's head. The Super Ball inspired him to call the championship game between the National Football League and the American Football League the "Super Bowl."

The Kansas City Chiefs lost the first Super Bowl.

21

How can **David Beckham** make a soccer ball "bend"?

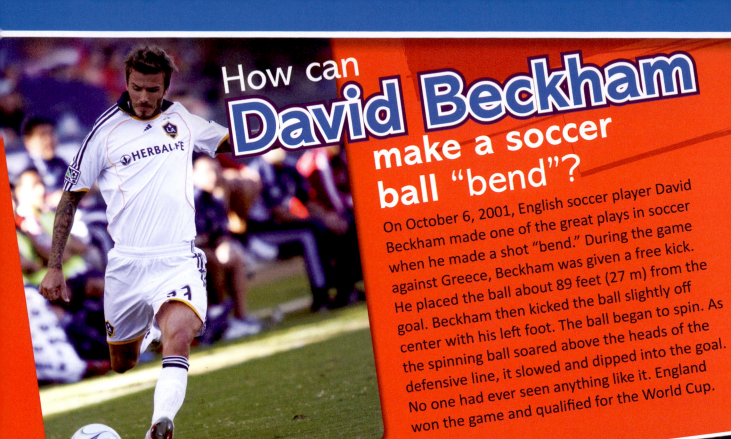

On October 6, 2001, English soccer player David Beckham made one of the great plays in soccer when he made a shot "bend." During the game against Greece, Beckham was given a free kick. He placed the ball about 89 feet (27 m) from the goal. Beckham then kicked the ball slightly off center with his left foot. The ball began to spin. As the spinning ball soared above the heads of the defensive line, it slowed and dipped into the goal. No one had ever seen anything like it. England won the game and qualified for the World Cup.

WHAT DOES A RED CARD MEAN IN SOCCER?

Soccer referees give players red cards for making serious fouls. Once the referee gives a player a red card, the player is removed from the game and cannot be replaced, leaving that team one player short. Two yellow cards also equal a red.

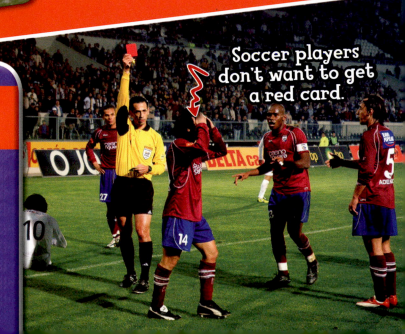

Soccer players don't want to get a red card.

WHY DO HOCKEY GOALIES WEAR MASKS?

Hockey goalies did not always wear face masks. In 1930, Clint Benedict, of the Montreal Maroons, first wore a mask in competition after a puck smashed into his face. He took the mask off after a few games. In 1959, Jacques Plante, the goaltender for the Montreal Canadiens, became the first goalie in NHL history to put on a face mask for good. Plante had been practicing with a fiberglass mask, but Canadien coach Toe Blake refused to allow Plante to wear it during the game. Three minutes into a game with the New York Rangers, a backhand shot split Plante's lip. He left for a few minutes, and returned wearing a mask.

Goaltender Jacques Plante wore the first hockey mask.

Today's hockey masks protect players better.

How can hockey players quickly speed up on the ice?

Professional hockey players can reach speeds of more than 20 miles (32 km) per hour on the ice. Friction is one of the reasons they move so fast. When a player begins skating, he digs the blade of one of his skates into the ice and pushes forward. The friction between the gripping blade and the slippery ice creates resistance. That resistance allows a player to exert more energy into moving forward.

23

Why do racehorses wear blinders?

When running a race, a horse often wears a mask over its head. No, they are not getting ready for Halloween. The masks, called blinders, block a horse's peripheral vision—the ability to see things out of the corner of the eye. This lets the animal focus all of its attention on the track in front of it.

WHY DO HORSES WEAR SHOES?

Just as your shoes protect the bottoms of your feet, horseshoes are designed to protect a horse's feet. Humans nail or glue the shoes onto the animal's hooves.

Horses wear shoes nailed to their hooves.

Why do racehorses run counterclockwise?

The reason dates back to the American Revolution. In 1780, William Whitley of Kentucky opened the first circular horse racetrack in America. A patriot, Whitley had the horses run counterclockwise to rebel against the British whose racehorses ran clockwise. Whitley's tradition remained when runners and cars took to the track.

Why does Michael **Phelps** wear a special swimsuit?

World-class swimmers such as Michael Phelps make swimming look easy. Phelps overcomes the effects of drag created by the water by being in great physical shape and by wearing a high-tech suit that allows water to flow over his body with less resistance.

Michael Phelps in a high-tech swim suit.

WHY IS MICHAEL PHELPS AN OLYMPIC SUPERSTAR?

Michael Phelps has won 14 career Olympic gold medals, the most by any Olympian. He also holds the record for winning the most gold medals in a single Olympics. He won eight at the 2008 Games in Beijing, China.

Janet Guthrie was a top female race car driver.

Who was the first woman to race in the Indianapolis 500?

Long before Danica Patrick became a famous race car driver, Janet Guthrie was the first woman to compete in the Indianapolis 500. The Indy 500 is one of racing's most important events. Guthrie raced in 1977. The year before, she also became the first woman to compete in NASCAR's Daytona 500.

WHO WAS THE FIRST FEMALE TO UMPIRE A MAJOR LEAGUE BASEBALL GAME?

"You're Ouuuuuuut!" In 1989, Pam Postema made history when she uttered those words. Postema was the first female to umpire a major league baseball game. The game was an exhibition and did not count. In 2007, Ria Cortesio became the second female umpire to work during a major league exhibition game. The game was between the Chicago Cubs and the Arizona Diamondbacks. No woman umpire has ever worked a regular-season game in the major leagues.

WHO WAS THE FIRST WOMAN TO ANNOUNCE AN NFL GAME?

In 1987, Gayle Sierens, a TV news anchor in Tampa, Florida, was the first woman to announce an NFL game. She was also the last. Sierens had once been a sportscaster. In the mid-1980s, an executive at NBC Sports thought a woman should call an NFL game. Sierens went to Missouri to broadcast a Seattle Seahawks–Kansas City Chiefs game. The reviews were good. NBC offered Sierens the opportunity to call six more games, but her bosses at the local TV station said she'd have to give up her anchor job if she accepted, so she turned down NBC's offer.

Which thoroughbred racehorse is the fastest of all time?

Secretariat has the honor of being the fastest racehorse of all time. In 1973, Secretariat ran in the Belmont Stakes by completing the 1½-mile (2.41 km) course in 2 minutes 24 seconds. When Secretariat crossed the finish line, he was an amazing 31 lengths ahead of his closest challengers. The horse had already won the Kentucky Derby with a time of 1 minute 59 seconds. Secretariat also won the Preakness, another famous race. The champion earned the Triple Crown, U.S. horse racing's greatest honor, for winning all three of those races in the same year.

Who is the fastest human?

In September 2009, Usain Bolt, from Jamaica, became the fastest human in the world. He ran the 100-meter dash in 9.58 seconds, shattering the old record of 9.69 seconds.

WHY WAS SECRETARIAT SO FAST?

Experts say that Secretariat was so fast because he had a 22-pound (9.97 kg) heart, more than twice the size of a typical thoroughbred's heart.

Why are there holes in Swiss cheese?

Raise your hand if you think mice chew the holes in Swiss cheese! Mice have nothing to do with the production of the cheese, but bacteria do. Bacteria are single-celled organisms that multiply very fast. All cheese is made by adding bacteria to milk. The milk begins to curdle as bacteria eat. Three types of bacteria help make Swiss cheese. Two types of bacteria produce lactic acid. The third type of bacteria lives off the lactic acid and gives off bubbles of carbon dioxide. Those bubbles form the holes that give Swiss cheese its unique look.

The holes in Swiss cheese comes from bursting bubbles.

Why aren't all bacteria bad for you?

While some bacteria can make a person sick, other bacteria are good for you. Some bacteria help in food digestion. Other types of bacteria live on skin and in the mouth to protect people from the bad bacteria that can make them sick.

Good bacteria are prime ingredients in making cheese.

WHY DOES CHEESE NEED TO AGE TO TASTE GOOD?

Age doesn't make everything better, but it sure improves a wheel of cheddar cheese! Some cheese is tastier when it is eaten at a very young age. However, some cheese is extremely yummy if it is left on the shelf for weeks or months. Aging allows the enzymes and bacteria in the cheese to transform it into a tasty snack. Each type of cheese requires a different aging period.

Why do leaves change color?

Red, orange, yellow, and brown—these are the colors of autumn. Trees make their own food through a process called **photosynthesis**. During photosynthesis, trees use the sun's light to turn water from the ground and carbon dioxide from the air into oxygen and **glucose**, a kind of sugar. Trees use glucose as food for energy. During the winter, there is not enough sunlight for photosynthesis. So, trees shut down their tiny food-making factories. When that happens, **chlorophyll** (needed for photosynthesis and to give leaves their green color) fades, leaving the leaves bright orange, red, and yellow.

When leaves fall, trees stop making food.

Why do leaves fall?

It is late autumn and all the leaves have fallen. As sunlight decreases in autumn, the hollow tubes that carry sap into and out of a leaf begin to close. As that happens, a layer of cells forms at the base of the leaf stem. Those cells help the leaf separate from the branch, and it falls to the ground.

WHY IS GRASS GREEN?

Grass is green because it is filled with chlorophyll. Chlorophyll is the green pigment that absorbs sunlight during photosynthesis.

29

Why is **water wet**?

Take a bath—get wet! Go for a swim—get wet! Get smacked in the noggin with a water balloon—get wet! Believe it or not, water isn't wet. Wetness is just a feeling we experience. In fact, liquids, such as water, aren't wet. Liquids have special qualities that make us feel "wet" when we touch them. When we change those qualities, water can be as hard as rock—think ice, or as light as air—think steam.

Why is water **tasteless**?

Like wetness, taste is a perception or experience brought to you by your taste buds. Taste buds allow people to taste things that are salty, sour, bitter, or sweet. Humans experience taste because molecules in food and drink interact with taste receptors in the mouth. Candy is sweet because the molecules in sugar react with our taste receptors. Water contains nothing to trigger our taste receptors. So, water seems to be tasteless to us. Drink up!

WHY IS WATER IMPORTANT FOR LIFE?

All life as we know it depends on water. Why is that? All the reactions that take place in our bodies to carry on life need a fluid to work. All living things use water to carry nutrients and other important chemicals to organs and cells. Water also helps our bodies flush out waste.

Without water, life as we know it would not exist.

Why do **chemical reactions occur?**

A chemical reaction occurs when two or more substances interact. Water forms when two hydrogen atoms react with one oxygen atom. An automobile rusts because iron atoms in the steel react with oxygen atoms in the air.

A chemical reaction causes water to form.

Hydrogen H_2

Oxygen O

Water H_2O

Why does mixing vinegar and baking soda cause an "explosion"?

How many times have you made a tabletop volcano? What do you use to give the volcano its pop? You use baking soda and vinegar, of course! When you mix vinegar and baking soda, a chemical reaction takes place. The acetic acid in vinegar—stuff that gives vinegar its sour taste—reacts with the sodium bicarbonate (a **compound** in baking soda) to form something entirely different— carbonic acid. Carbonic acid breaks down into carbon dioxide and water. The escaping carbon dioxide gas creates the bubbles you see as they overflow like a gushing volcano.

HOW IS A GAS DIFFERENT FROM A SOLID OR LIQUID?

Matter, which is anything that has mass and takes up space, comes in three states: solid, gas, and liquid. An ice cube is a solid. Solids have tightly packed particles. Helium is a gas. In a gas, particles move fast and don't stay close together. Water is a liquid. Liquid particles move around, but don't have a shape.

31

Why does a bee make honey?

Bees buzz near blooming flowers to find sweet nectar. A single honeybee will visit between 50 and 100 flowers on one trip. Bees take the nectar and turn it into honey. Bees store honey in hives to eat later when flowers are not blooming.

Why do **bees dance?**

Bees dance to communicate with each other. Scout bees, for example, look for flower beds bursting with pollen. If they find one, they fly to the hive and "dance" to tell the other bees what they found. Some bees also dance the "round dance" to tell other bees that pollen is near the hive.

Thousands of bees can live in one hive.

Bees help create new plants.

WHY DO BEES POLLINATE FLOWERS?

As bees look for food, they help create new plants through **pollination**. Bees take pollen from the male parts of a flower and move it to the female parts of a flower. The flower then creates a seed. From that seed a new plant grows. In the United States, bees pollinate 95 different crops.

Why does a pencil look like it's **bending in water?**

If you hold a pencil straight up in a glass of water and look through the side of the glass, it looks as though the pencil is bending. Light is playing tricks on your eyes. When light beams enter water, the water slows down the beams of light. This causes the light to bend away from its original path, a process called **refraction**.

Light can play tricks on your eyes.

Why does it look like there's **water** on a road when it is **sunny outside?**

Drive down the road on a hot summer day, and you might see a puddle of water in the middle of the street even though it has not rained. The puddle is a mirage, or vision caused by bending light. A light beam can change direction, or bend, when it passes from cooler air to hotter air. On a hot sunny day, the road's pavement is warmer than the air above it. When light hits the boundary between the cooler and warmer air, it bends just enough to make a "puddle" seem to appear on the roadway.

WHY DO SOME PEOPLE SNEEZE IF THEY LOOK INTO THE SUN?

Have you ever come from a dark room into the bright sunshine and started to sneeze? You might suffer from photic sneeze reflex, which causes people to sneeze in the sudden appearance of bright light, especially sunlight. No one knows exactly why the reflex exists. Some scientists think the cause is located in a person's nervous system.

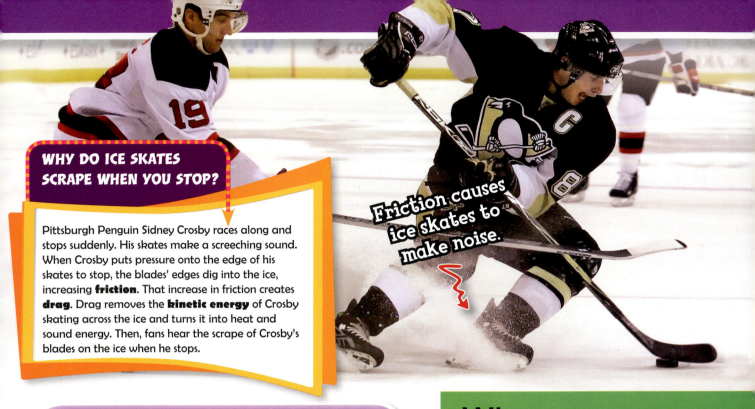

WHY DO ICE SKATES SCRAPE WHEN YOU STOP?

Pittsburgh Penguin Sidney Crosby races along and stops suddenly. His skates make a screeching sound. When Crosby puts pressure onto the edge of his skates to stop, the blades' edges dig into the ice, increasing **friction**. That increase in friction creates **drag**. Drag removes the **kinetic energy** of Crosby skating across the ice and turns it into heat and sound energy. Then, fans hear the scrape of Crosby's blades on the ice when he stops.

Friction causes ice skates to make noise.

WHY DOES SALT MELT ICE?

When the temperature is below 32°F (0°C), water freezes into ice. Since salt water doesn't freeze until a slightly lower temperature, adding salt to an icy sidewalk or road can melt ice, as long as the temperature isn't lower than the freezing point of salt water.

Why can we skate on ice?

Although the question seems simple enough, scientists are still searching for an answer. They used to believe that ice under a skate is slippery because the pressure of the skate's blade lowers the melting temperature of the ice surface. As the ice melts, the blade glides across the thin layer of water. That water refreezes as soon as the blade passes. Some scientists now believe that water molecules on the surface of ice vibrate faster because nothing is holding them down. As a result, the molecules remain unfrozen, making ice slippery.

Why does baking soda get rid of odors in the fridge?

Because no one wants to smell last night's fish dinner, people often put a box of baking soda in the fridge to soak up the smell. Odors, such as those from sour milk, are created by acids in the food. Molecules of these acids rise up in the air, causing the odor. Baking soda absorbs these acid molecules and neutralizes them, removing the odor. However, over time the powder becomes less effective, especially when it mixes with water vapor. A crust forms on top of the powder, limiting the baking soda's ability to soak up the smell.

WHY DON'T SWEATY HANDS SMELL AS BAD AS SWEATY FEET?

Feet smell because they sweat. In fact, there are more than 250,000 sweat glands in feet. Bacteria feed off the salt and water of sweat. The bacteria then give off waste, which causes a nose-numbing odor on shoes and socks. Although hands have the same number of sweat glands as feet do, they are not usually wrapped in socks and shoes. Sweat evaporates on hands before bacteria can feed, whereas sweat on feet cannot evaporate as quickly.

Why does my breath smell?

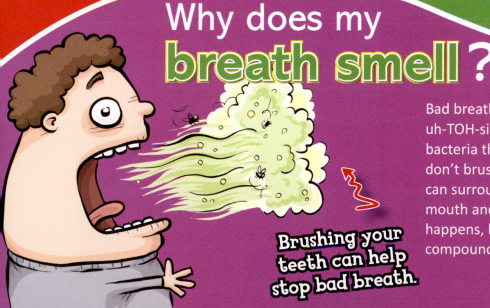

Brushing your teeth can help stop bad breath.

Bad breath, also known as halitosis (hal-uh-TOH-sis), is caused by odor-producing bacteria that grow in your mouth. If you don't brush or floss regularly, the bacteria can surround bits of food left in your mouth and between your teeth. When that happens, bacteria release smelly sulfur compounds, which make your breath stink.

35

Why does eating a hot pepper **burn my tongue**?

If you have ever bitten into a jalapeño or a chili pepper, you probably felt pain because it was so hot. Hot peppers are steamy because they contain capsaicin (cap-SAY-sin). Capsaicin is a pepper plant's natural defense against animals that might want to eat it. Birds, however, aren't affected by capsaicin. That's a good thing, because birds help spread the plant's seeds so more pepper plants can grow.

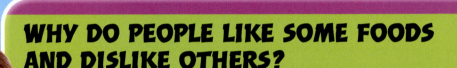

WHY DO PEOPLE LIKE SOME FOODS AND DISLIKE OTHERS?

Scientists say genetics play a role in why we like some foods and not others. Researchers say our genes decide the number of taste buds we have on our tongues. A Yale University researcher says that people with more taste buds can experience the taste, texture, and temperature of food better than those with fewer taste buds. As such, the more taste buds a person has, the more foods that person will probably enjoy.

The Swiss eat the most chocolate in the world, about 22 pounds per person each year.

Why can eating chocolate candy **make people hyper?**

Chocolate candy and many soft drinks contain sugar and caffeine. It's the caffeine, not the sugar, that can make a person jumpy or hyper. Some parents blame sugar for their children's **hyperactivity**. But most researchers now say that sugar does not make most children "bounce off the wall." Some studies show that artificial, or human-made, food dyes are responsible for increased hyperactivity in kids.

Why do helium balloons float?

Up, up, and away! If you have ever let go of a helium-filled balloon at a fair or a birthday party, you know that the balloon floats away. Why? Helium is a gas that is lighter than the surrounding air. The balloon rises because the helium displaces, or pushes away, the air around the balloon. This is known as **buoyancy**. Balloons are a danger to wildlife, especially sea creatures, so don't let balloons float away!

Why does a spoon get hot in a pot of **boiling water?**

A process called **conduction** is the reason that heat energy travels from a pot of boiling water to a spoon sitting in the pot. During conduction, the molecules in the hot water are moving quickly. They pass heat to other molecules around them. In time, they pass heat to the spoon sitting in the pot.

The helium in balloons is lighter than the air.

HOW DO ICE CUBES MAKE DRINKS COLDER?

As ice absorbs the heat from a drink, the ice gets warmer and begins to melt and turns into water. The cooler water from the ice makes the drink colder. The more ice you put in a drink, the quicker the ice absorbs the heat.

How do **clouds form?**

Clouds form when the sun warms air containing water vapor. As warm air rises, it becomes colder. Gradually the water vapor in the air turns into tiny drops of water. The molecules in the water grab hold of tiny bits of dust, pollen, and other types of pollution. Clouds form as the water molecules condense onto these particles.

HOW LARGE CAN SOME S IOWFLAKES BE?

As snow hits the ground, the average snowflake is about 0.5 inches (1.3 cm) across. If the falling ice crystals stick together, some flakes can measure more than 4 inches (10 cm) across and be made up of as many as 100 separate ice crystals.

How does **snow form?**

Snow begins its life as an ice crystal. Ice crystals form when the temperature in a cloud is below freezing, 32°F (0°C). If the temperature of the air just below the cloud is also below freezing, the crystals cling together and fall to the ground as snowflakes.

Why does laundry **detergent** **remove dirt from clothes?**

Laundry detergents are made up of chains of carbon and hydrogen molecules. While some of those molecules love water, some of them hate water. When you put detergent in the washing machine with dirty clothes, the water-hating soap molecules bind to the dirt. When you turn the washing machine on, it swirls the water. This allows the soapy water around the dirt to pull the grime away from the clothes.

Why does dish soap clean greasy plates?

Dish soap molecules are made up of long chains. One end of the chain attaches itself to the grease on the dinner plate, prying the scum loose. The grease is then carried off by rinsing with water.

Detergent contains water-hating molecules.

WHY DOES OIL FLOAT ON WATER?

Try this experiment: Pour a few drops of vegetable oil into a glass of water. The oil floats on top of the water, spreads out, and makes a light covering. Why? First, most oils weigh less than water. Second, most oils do not dissolve in water, but tend to stick together. When oil goes into water, oil molecules cluster near each other at the surface.

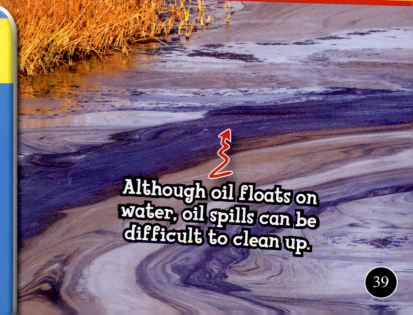

Although oil floats on water, oil spills can be difficult to clean up.

What is that big red spot we see when we look at **Jupiter** through **a telescope?**

Jupiter's Great Red Spot is an ancient storm resembling a hurricane on Earth. No one knows why the storm is red. All they know is that the storm has been raging for more than 300 years—that's how long humans have been observing Jupiter through telescopes. Jupiter's red spot is big enough to hold three Earths. Scientists say that Jupiter's red spot, however, is shrinking.

Jupiter's red spot will one day disappear.

Why is a year on Jupiter much longer **than a year on Earth?**

Did you know if you're 13 years old on Jupiter, you would be about 156 years old on Earth? A year on Jupiter is equal to almost 12 years on Earth. In other words, it takes Jupiter 12 Earth years to go once around the sun. The days on Jupiter are much shorter than the days on Earth, however. It takes Jupiter just 9.8 hours to rotate completely on its axis, while it takes Earth 24 hours.

You can see Jupiter's bands through a small telescope.

WHY ARE THERE BANDS AROUND JUPITER?

The colorful bands around Jupiter are evidence of complex weather systems. The light-colored bands are named "zones," while the dark-colored bands are called "belts." High-speed winds blow the belts and zones in opposite directions, causing multicolored patterns to form. The colors come from the tiny chemical and temperature differences between the neighboring bands.

Why does temperature change?

Temperature is a degree of hotness or coldness that we measure using a thermometer. Temperature is related to how fast the molecules of a substance are moving. The faster the molecules move, the higher the temperature. So molecules in boiling water move much faster than those in ice water. Molecules slow down as the hot water cools, bringing the temperature from hotter to cooler.

WHY IS IT HOTTER AT THE EQUATOR THAN AT THE NORTH AND SOUTH POLES?

The sun's rays warm the Earth. Although there is the same amount of solar radiation hitting the Earth at the poles and at the equator, the sun's rays fall more directly on the equator than on the poles. That is because of Earth's curvature, or rounded shape. This is why temperatures at the equator are much warmer than temperatures in the Arctic or Antarctica.

This lion lives in Kenya, a nation in Africa that straddles the equator.

WHY IS IT COOLER ON TOP OF A MOUNTAIN THAN AT ITS BASE?

Air is made of billions of tiny air molecules. Gravity holds those molecules close to Earth's surface. The sun's rays first heat Earth's surface. That heat then radiates up, warming the surrounding air molecules. Air molecules are less able to store heat energy the higher they go. So, it is much cooler at the top of a mountain than near its base.

It's frosty at the top of a mountain.

41

Why does glue have **sticky properties**?

Glue has two properties that make it sticky: adhesion and cohesion. Adhesion is the glue's ability to hold objects together. Cohesion is the glue's ability to hold on to itself. These two properties help glue stick to surfaces by seeping into the cracks and holes of an object's surface and then hardening and locking on to that surface.

WHY IS TAPE STICKY?

Tape is a band of flexible material treated on one or both sides with temporary glue that can stick to surfaces.

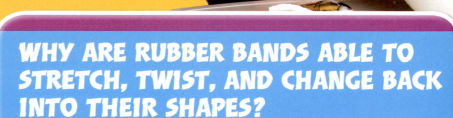

Glue has two properties that make it sticky.

Rubber bands stretch because of chains of stringy molecules.

WHY ARE RUBBER BANDS ABLE TO STRETCH, TWIST, AND CHANGE BACK INTO THEIR SHAPES?

That quality is known as elasticity. Rubber contains carbon and hydrogen. Rubber bands are stretchy because the molecules of these elements bond together into long, flexible chains called polymers. Pulling a rubber band causes the polymers to untwist and straighten. When you release the rubber band, the polymers return to their original form.

How did e-mail start?

You've got mail! People send billions of e-mails by using the Internet. The first person to send an e-mail, or electronic mail, was Ray Tomlinson. In 1971, Tomlinson was working on a computer system that would later become the Internet. He found he needed a better way to leave messages on the computers of his fellow workers. He used the @ sign to separate names of users from names of their computers on the **network**. So, today we address e-mails like this: janedoe@earthlink.net.

E-mails can travel around the globe in seconds.

Why do some e-mails bounce back?

Sometimes you send a person an e-mail and it "bounces" back to you. When your e-mail system makes contact with someone's e-mail server, the server decides if it will let the message through. If it doesn't, the server bounces the message back. Why? Perhaps the address is wrong. It may be misspelled. There may not be enough room on the system, or an e-mail system may fail.

WHAT DOES *HTTP* MEAN?

The Internet is a very complex system that connects millions of computers to one another. In 1989, a British scientist named Tim Berners-Lee invented hypertext transfer protocol, or http, a series of linked words that allows users to navigate the Internet. In short, Berners-Lee invented the first Web browser.

"Please turn off all electronic devices, including cell phones and computers." If you have ever flown in an airplane, you have heard those words. Flight attendants always make sure passengers in flight do not use their cell phones when the plane is taking off or landing.

What's the reason for this? Airplanes contain many radios that do a lot of different things. One type of radio allows pilots to talk to ground control. Another type lets air traffic controllers know where the plane is located. Cell phone transmissions can interfere with how these radios work, especially if the cell phones are on the same radio frequency as the plane's equipment. If that happens, it is possible the cell phone signals could create equipment problems within the plane.

HOW ARE CELL PHONES LIKE TINY RADIOS?

Cell phones send and receive radio signals. Their networks are divided into "cells." Cells are geographic areas that have a special station to receive and send radio signals. Each station has an **antenna**, more commonly known as a cell phone tower. The antenna transmits signals just like a radio station. When you turn on your cell phone, it searches for a signal from the nearest cell phone tower. If you're too far away from a tower, or if the signal is too faint, you will lose the signal…and the call.

What do **3G** and **4G** stand for with cell phones?

The phrase 3G network is short for third generation network. That means 3G networks are more advanced than the previous network. The phrase 4G network is short for fourth generation network. You can send large amounts of data on 3G and 4G networks, but 4G networks are faster than 3G networks. Smart phones use both 3G and 4G networks depending on the carrier.

How are HDTVs and standard TVs different?

HDTV stands for high-definition television. HDTVs work by picking up and decoding digital signals. When a TV station broadcasts in high definition, the station changes pictures and sounds into trillions of bits of electronic data. An HDTV takes that digital data and changes it back into pictures and sounds. A standard TV turns radio signals into sounds and pictures. Radio signals do not carry as much information as digital signals.

WHY DO DIGITAL MOVIE PROJECTORS HAVE SHARPER PICTURES THAN STANDARD PROJECTORS?

Digital light processing, or DLP, will soon be coming to a theater near you. Instead of using film, DLP projectors show pictures and play back sound that were previously digitized, or converted, into trillions of bits of information. Digital projectors bounce light off millions of tiny mirrors onto a movie screen, producing a crystal-clear picture with high-quality sound.

HDTVs are becoming more popular and are quickly replacing standard TVs.

Why is HDTV **clearer and sharper** than standard TV?

HDTVs have more lines of information and pixels (tiny colored dots) per square inch than standard TVs, resulting in a clearer picture that is much sharper than a standard, television.

45

Web sites

Animals
The Animal Planet's http://animal.discovery.com/ is neat. There are games, videos, and blogs.

Earth
Take a wonderful journey across the globe with this Web site from the Smithsonian Institution: http://www.mnh.si.edu/earth/main_frames.html.

Space
NASA's Web sites are out of this world. Check out http://solarsystem.nasa.gov/planets/index.cfm and learn more about our solar system. Click on a planet and discover amazing facts.

Humans
Go to http://kidshealth.org/kid/htbw/htbw_main_page.html and learn how the human body works.

People and Places
Explore the world on http://www.nationalgeographic.com/. This amazing Web site links to parts of the world many people don't know about. You can access news features, maps, and videos and learn about many different people and places. For the latest news about people and places, go to timeforkids.com.

History
If you're a history buff, go to http://www.history.com/. Click on "This Day in History" to find out what happened on any particular day. Learn about world leaders and play dozens of games.

Science
Read more about the world of science with National Geographic at http://science.nationalgeographic.com/science/.

Technology
If you're interested in some of the dumbest inventions ever produced, the editors of *Life* magazine have put them all together for you at http://www.life.com/image/3270485/in-gallery/25371.

Arts and Culture
If you're interested in the art of the Renaissance, http://www.renaissanceconnection.org/home.html is a wonderful place to learn about how Renaissance artists lived and worked.

Sports
Sports and kids go together like, well, sports and kids. Keep up with all the news of sports and play some games at http://www.sikids.com/.

Book List

Animals
National Geographic Encyclopedia of Animals by Karen McGhee & George McKay, PhD (National Geographic Society, 2006)

Earth
Smithsonian Earth by James F. Luhr (Dorling Kindersley Publishing, 2007)

Space
Smithsonian Atlas of Space Exploration by Roger D. Launius & Andrew K. Johnston (Smithsonian Institution, 2009)

Humans
Human Body: An Interactive Guide to the Inner Workings of the Body (Barron's Educational Series, 2008)

People and Places
History of the World: People, Places, and Ideas by Henry Billing (Steck-Vaughn Company, 2003)

History
Children's Encyclopedia of American History by David C. King (Smithsonian Institution, 2003)

Science
*The Science Book: Everything You Need to Know About the World and How It Work*s by Marshall Brain (National Geographic, 2008)

Technology
Computers and Technology by Tara Koellhoffer, (Editor) & Emily Sohn (Forward) (Chelsea Clubhouse, 2006)

Arts and Culture
Performing Arts (Culture Encyclopedia) by Antony Mason (Mason Crest Publishers, 2002)

Sports
The Greatest Moments in Sports by Len Berman (Sourcebooks, 2009)

aerodynamics the forces exerted by air or other gases in motion

antenna a metallic device used for sending and receiving radio waves

buoyancy the ability of an object to float or rise when submerged in a fluid

chlorophyll the green pigment in plants responsible for the absorption of light energy during photosynthesis

compounds the combination of two or more elements

conduction the movement of heat energy from one object to another

drag the resistance to a moving body created by rushing air or water

friction the force that one surface exerts on another when the two rub against each other

glucose sugar in plants that is used as food for energy

hyperactivity unusually active

integrated open to everyone regardless of race

kinetic energy the energy of movement

matter anything that has mass and can be measured; There are three types of matter: solids, liquids, and gases.

network two or more computers that are linked by wires or cables

photosynthesis the process by which green plants trap light and energy to form carbohydrates

pollination the transfer of individual pollen grains from the male part of a plant to the female part of the plant that makes fertilization possible

potential energy stored energy

refraction bending of a light wave